INVENTIONS IN

THE
Clothing Industry

THIS BOOK BELONGS TO:

Debra J. Housel

Table of Contents

In Your Closet

You look in your closet and say, "Mom, I don't have a thing to wear! Can we go shopping?"

You may spend hours in the store choosing *garments* (GAHR-muhnts). You want to wear clothes that make you look and feel good. But where do all those clothes come from? Who made them, and how?

Let's find out.

Jeans

If you're like most people, you have some jeans. Levi Strauss invented them for gold miners in 1873. Today's jeans look much like the first pairs. The pockets still have copper *rivets* (RIV-its). Strauss added them to make the pockets strong so miners could carry gold.

Denim and Levi's

The dark blue cloth used to make jeans is called *denim*. The first denim came from Genoa, Italy. Some people said "jeans" for Genoa, and the name stuck. Can you tell where Levi's got their name? From Levi Strauss, of course!

Raincoats

If you own a raincoat, you can thank Charles Macintosh. He made the first waterproof cloth. He put a thin rubber coating on two pieces of cloth. He pressed the pieces together with the rubber in between. The rubber stuck together. He made the cloth into raincoats. People loved them! They could stay dry when it rained.

◄ Macintosh made the world's first raincoat in 1823.

Pockets

No one knows just who invented pockets. Late in the 1500s, a tailor put a slit in men's pants. A man tied his money bag to his belt and hid it behind the slit. Over time the slit changed to a pocket. Before long everyone wanted pockets.

◄ Each year people buy more than 425 million pairs of jeans worldwide.

◀ A cobbler makes shoes for each individual customer.

◀ 16th century leather shoes

Uppers and Soles

An upper is the top of the shoe. A sole is the bottom.

Shoes

Years ago, *cobblers* made shoes for people when they ordered them. After he measured the person's foot, he chose the shoe form that matched. The cobbler used the form to cut leather *uppers* and *soles*. He sewed together the pieces of the uppers. Finally, he used tiny wooden pegs to attach the uppers and soles. All of this took days.

▼ A factory can turn out hundreds of pairs of shoes daily.

Left or Right?

Until the early 1800s, there was no difference between right and left shoes! Then, cobblers started using right and left forms, which made shoes much more comfortable.

Today shoe pieces are mainly cut and put together on machines. Some shoes are stitched and others glued. This makes shoes cost less so people can afford more pairs.

Fasteners

Zippers

Zippers were first made in 1893 for high-topped shoes. Whitcomb Judson called his creation a "clasp locker and unlocker for shoes." Thirty years later, the B. F. Goodrich Company made a change to the design. They used teeth instead of hooks on their "Zipper Boots." Soon zippers were added to other garments.

You probably have many things in your closet with zippers.

▼ THEN–Judson zipper   ▼ NOW–Modern zipper

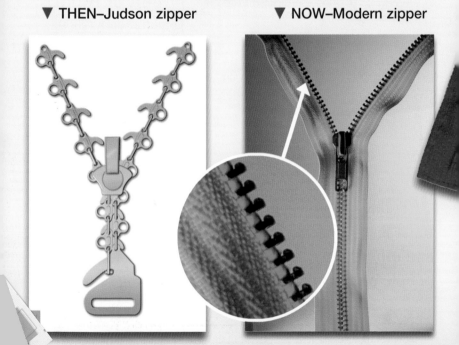

Velcro

Do you have shoes or boots with Velcro straps? The inventor got the idea after burrs stuck to his pants. Velcro is *nylon* tape. One side is covered with tiny loops. The other side has tiny hooks. When closed, the hooks grab the loops, just as burrs grab cloth or fur. Pulling on the hooks releases them.

Georges de Mestral invented Velcro. ▼

Fastener Time Line

By looking at old paintings and statues, we know when different clothing *fasteners* first appeared.

Fastener (FAS-uhn-er)	When People Started Using Them
button ▶	first used before written history and fastened with loops until buttonholes were invented
buckle ▶	400s
eyelet with laces	1000s
buttonhole	1200s
◀ hook and eye	1600s *(sailors)*
safety pin ▶	1849 *(Walter Scott)*
snap	1850s
◀ zipper	1893 *(Whitcomb Judson)*
Velcro	1956 *(Georges de Mestral)*

Inventors

The inventors' names for most fasteners have been forgotten. If the inventor's name is known, it is given on the chart.

▲ American Puritans used only hooks-and-eyes or buckles on their clothes. They believed that buttons were sinful.

Fabrics and Fibers

Do you have a favorite thing to wear? The *fabric* may be one reason it's your favorite.

Some fabrics are made of *natural fibers*. Natural fibers come from plants and animals. Long ago people learned how to make these fibers into cloth. First, *carding* untangles the fibers. Then, the fibers are twisted into thread. In the past, this was always done with a *spinning wheel.* The thread gathers on a spool. Then, the threads are put on a *loom* and woven into fabric. This cloth is cut and sewn to form clothes.

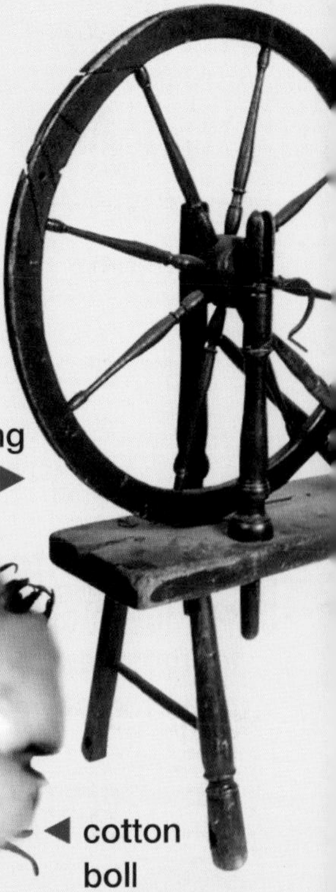

spinning wheel ▶

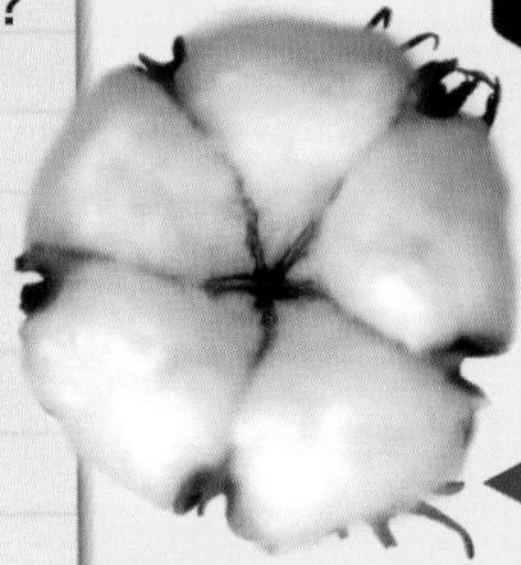

◀ cotton boll

Knitting

Thick thread, or yarn, can be *knit* into clothing, too. When did people first knit? Probably about three thousand years ago! We think the first knitters lived in the Arabian Desert of Egypt. The first knitting machine was invented in 1864.

Cotton is the most-used fiber. When the cotton's flowers change to bolls of white fluff, it gets picked. The seeds are removed. Then the cotton is cleaned and spun into thread. The thread is woven into cloth on a loom.

At one time all this was done by hand. That took a long time! Then Eli Whitney invented the *cotton gin*. It removed the seeds from the bolls. Later cotton picking machines and faster, better looms were invented, too

▲ Eli Whitney

Did You Know?

The words *cotton gin* really come from *cotton engine*. The word engine was just shortened over time.

▲ Fibers are made into cloth using looms.

Kevlar

Kevlar is a manmade fabric that is used for protection. It can protect firefighters and racecar drivers from heat. When layered, it can make bulletproof vests to protect police officers.

Did you know that you might have clothes made from recycled soda bottles? It's true if you own *microfleece*. This soft, fluffy fabric comes from melted plastic bottles.

Microfleece is a recent *synthetic* (sin-THET-ik) fabric. Synthetic means manmade. In 1884, a chemist made *rayon*, the first manmade fiber, from wood chips. Chemicals change the chips into a thick liquid. The fluid is shot through tiny metal holes called *spinnerets*. It lands in an acid bath and hardens. Then, the fibers are twisted into thread.

spinnerets

Amazing!

The next time you toss a soda bottle into your recycle bin, remember it may become a shirt, scarf, or hat!

▲ a microfiber hat

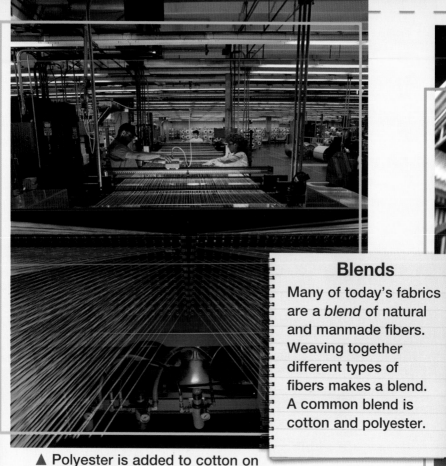

Blends

Many of today's fabrics are a *blend* of natural and manmade fibers. Weaving together different types of fibers makes a blend. A common blend is cotton and polyester.

▲ Polyester is added to cotton on a loom. It reduces wrinkling.

Scientists wanted to invent more fibers, so they kept working. In the 1930s and 1940s, they invented nylon and *polyester*. Both come from *petroleum* (puh-TROH-lee-uhm). These fabrics are made in the same way as rayon. Their fibers stretch, so they're often used in sports clothes and swimsuits.

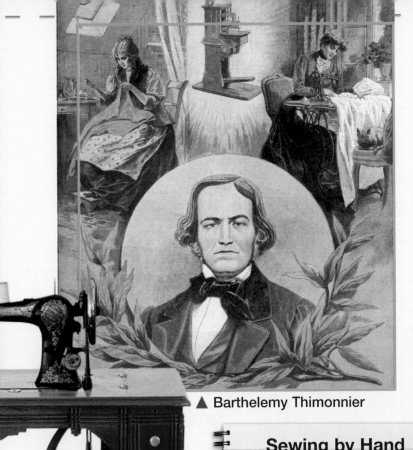

▲ Barthelemy Thimonnier

treadle

Sewing by Hand

People have been sewing by hand for more than 20,000 years. The first sewing needles were made of bones or animal horns. The first thread was made of animal *sinew*. Do you know how to sew by hand?

Isaac Singer made the first electric sewing machine in 1889. Now, *assembly line* clothing could be made rapidly. Since clothes could be made faster, they could be made more cheaply, too. Clothes went straight from factories to stores. People were glad not to have to make all their own clothes anymore.

Assembly line sewing let clothes be made faster than ever before. ▼

▲ a modern assembly line

▲ an assembly line from the early 1900s

Machines Time Line

Here are some of the most useful machines in clothing history.

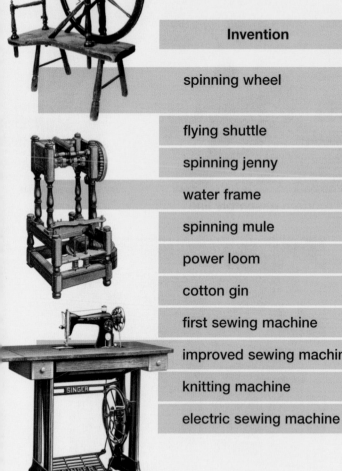

Invention	Year
spinning wheel	1000s
flying shuttle	1733
spinning jenny	1764
water frame	1769
spinning mule	1779
power loom	1785
cotton gin	1793
first sewing machine	1830
improved sewing machine	1846
knitting machine	1864
electric sewing machine	1889

Inventor

oldest found in India, inventor unknown

John Kay

James Hargreaves

Richard Arkwright

Samuel Crompton

Edmund Cartwright

Eli Whitney

Barthelemy Thimonnier

Elias Howe

William Cotton

Isaac Singer

What's in Store?

What's in store for the clothing industry? Scientists want to change the genes of some plants. Then, they will grow polyester-like fibers. When this new kind of fabric gets thrown out, it will rot and eventually turn into dirt.

There's always something happening in the world of clothing. *Fashions* change with time. *Designers* change styles, making people want new and different garments. Two hundred years ago, no one would have dreamed of something like blue jeans. Can you imagine what your great-grandchildren will be wearing?

Glossary

assembly line   a way of making a piece of clothing or other item so that the jobs are divided among many people

carding   to untangle fibers before spinning them, using a wire-toothed brush or machine with rows of wire teeth

cobbler   a person who makes shoes

designers   people who create new clothing styles

fabric   cloth

fashions   clothing styles

fasteners   the things that hold shoes or garments closed

fibers   long, thin, thread-like objects

flying shuttle   a machine that carries the thread from side to side through other threads that run lengthwise on a loom

garments   pieces of clothing

knit   to connect yarn or thread in a series of loops, either by hand, with knitting needles, or on a machine

loom   a machine used to make cloth by weaving thread or yarn together

petroleum   crude oil before it has been refined (separated into natural gas, oil, kerosene, etc); also the basis for gasoline

power loom   a loom that operates automatically by steam or electrical power

ready-made   already made and on a store shelf or rack before the customer goes to purchase it

rivets   metal pieces used to hold two sides of something together

sinew   the stringy, tough, cord of an animal that connects a muscle to a bone

spinneret   tiny holes through which plastic material is sprayed

spinning jenny   a machine that spins several spools of thread at the same time

spinning mule   a mechanical spinning wheel that spins 1,000 spools of thread at the same time

spinning wheel   a machine made of a wheel that is driven by hand or foot and used to make fibers into thread

synthetic   invented and made by people instead of growing from nature

tailor   person whose job it is to make and repair clothes

Index